D1796431

CONTENTS

My Legacy

What I Will Be Remembered For

Rt. Hon. David Cameron

ISBN: 1542564727
ISBN-13: 978-1542564724

I had other plans, initially.

ACKNOWLEDGMENTS

To George, for sinking on the ship with me.

Thanks, and no thanks, to Boris and Michael.

1. MY POLITICAL LEGACY

Accidentally leaving the EU.

My Legacy

Rt. Hon. David Cameron

2. MY ECONOMIC LEGACY

Accidentally leaving the EU.

Rt. Hon. David Cameron

My Legacy

3. MY INTELLECTUAL LEGACY

Accidentally leaving the EU.

My Legacy

Rt. Hon. David Cameron

4. MY PARTY LEGACY

Accidentally leaving the EU.

My Legacy

Rt. Hon. David Cameron

5. MY HISTORICAL LEGACY

Abolishing poverty.

Just kidding.

I accidentally took the UK out of the EU.

My Legacy

Rt. Hon. David Cameron

6. MY 'CHURCHILL MOMENT'

Accidentally leaving the EU.

Rt. Hon. David Cameron

7. MY SOCIAL LEGACY

'Big society.'

Well. It should have been.

I accidentally took the UK out of the EU, instead.

Rt. Hon. David Cameron

My Legacy

8. MY MISTAKE

Tough one. Probably leaving the EU, entirely by accident.

Rt. Hon. David Cameron

Rt. Hon. David Cameron

9. WHAT I WOULD HAVE DONE DIFFERENTLY

I regret nothing. History will recognise my genius.

Rt. Hon. David Cameron

My Legacy

10. WHAT I WILL DO NEXT.

Help advise on how we can accidentally get the best deal from the EU in trade agreements.

My Legacy

ABOUT THE AUTHOR

The Right Honourable David Cameron was the Prime Minister of the United Kingdom from May 2010 until July 2016.

Just 6 years, such a shame.

But what can you do? Best laid plans of mice and men, and all that.

Printed in Great
Britain
by Amazon

31439298R00031